T0023994

YOUR VOTE MATTERS

HOW WE ELECT THE US PRESIDENT

Written by Rebecca Katzman

Illustrated by Ellen Duda

SCHOLASTIC INC.

CONTENTS

The Basics

Your Vote (and Voice) Matters! 4

Who Needs Government Anyway? .6

It's in the Constitution! 8

The Three Branches of Government 10

Presenting the President. 12

Who Can Vote? 14

Fighting for Your Right 15

So You Want to Be President? 20

Running for President

The Long and Winding Road to the White House. 24

It's (Political) Party Time! 26

Show Your Primary Colors. 29

Picking the Vice President 34

It's a Party for Your Party! 38

Hop Aboard the Campaign Train 41

The Great Debates. 50

Issues of the Day 55

How Do You Pick Who to Vote For? 58

Get Out the Vote

It's Election Day! 60

Voting Way Back When. 61

Show Up and Vote! 63

Suppressing the Vote 64

The Cold Hard Truth About Gerrymandering 68

Behold the Ballot 70

Other Ways to Vote 72

A Peek Inside the Polling Place 74

And the Next President Is . . .

The Votes Pour In 76

The Electoral College 77

Blue States, Red States, and Purple States. 81

Election Shocks and Surprises 83

Good Winners and Losers 88

The Great Transition 89

Let's Get Inaugurated! 90

Life in the White House

The President Hard at Work. 92

The First Lady (or First Gentleman) 94

The President's Dream Team 96

Nobody's Above the Law. 100

Life After Office. 102

Your Vote Matters!

You Can Make a Difference. 104

Presidents of the United States 106

Glossary. 108

Index 110

Look for underlined **GLOSSARY WORDS** throughout this book to look up more info!

★ THE BASICS ★

YOUR VOTE (AND VOICE) MATTERS!

Welcome to the United States—our GREAT, WONDERFUL, and FABULOUS <u>DEMOCRACY</u>. What exactly is a democracy, you ask? It isn't a place where you can just push your way into power and declare yourself president. Instead, **we the people** get to vote for the person we think will do the best job.

Voting is one of the coolest things you can do as a US citizen. And it's not that hard, either. On Election Day, you go to your local <u>POLLING PLACE</u> and cast a vote for the person you think has what it takes to run the country.

There's just one catch: You won't be able to vote in elections until you're eighteen years old. But your voice still counts! There's a lot you can do to make a difference while you're growing up. Plus, it's important to learn how elections work. This way, you'll be able to step up and play your part as soon as you're old enough to vote.

You can change history simply by showing up and **casting a <u>BALLOT</u>**. That's right: The power to shape the future is in your hands. That's a lot of responsibility, so it's important to be an informed voter. And here in the United States, there's A LOT to be informed about. The process of electing the president of the United States can get a little complicated. It takes a lot of steps to get from your own house to the White House.

Ready to cruise down the long and winding road to **1600 Pennsylvania Avenue**? Buckle up, let's go!

Psst, that's the White House!

CAMPAIGNING

VOTE for ME!

★ A ★ BETTER FUTURE ★

INAUGURATION DAY

THE WHITE HOUSE!

VOTE HERE

ELECTION DAY

What is government—and why do we need it? Try picturing a world without stoplights or speed limits. Without the government, there would be no laws, so anybody could commit a crime. There would be nobody around to put out fires or collect the garbage, either. Everyone would have to fend for themselves.

A world without government wouldn't be a very fun or safe place to live. The government pays for our schools, builds our highways, and gives money and help to those who need it. The people we elect make and enforce laws. They help decide what's fair and what's not fair. They work to make the country a better and safer place.

The government has a hand in creating ALL these places.

fire station

police station

library

courthouse

school

The United States is a special type of government called a **democracy**. That means citizens have a say in the decisions that will affect their lives. It also means citizens elect the people in power. We do this by voting!

Elections are a fair way to make decisions as a group. The results are usually decided by the **majority**. That's the choice of more than half of the people voting.

And guess what? The people we elect to office work for *us*— the citizens of the country. We tell them how to run the nation with our voices and our votes.

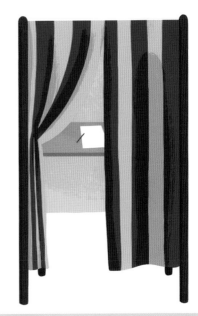

IT'S A FACT

We hold elections for many different positions in the government, not just for president. For example, we elect people to run our states (like governors) and our cities, too (like mayors).

Zoom back in time over two hundred years. Picture a bunch of men gathered in a crowded hall, working together to create a document. These men were our Founding Fathers, and that document was the US <u>CONSTITUTION</u>. The Constitution gives the basic rules for our country and explains how our government works.

It was written in 1787!

The Founding Fathers decided we would have a president who would be **elected**, or chosen, by the voters. Not every country picks their leaders this way. Before the United States was formed in 1776, Great Britain controlled the original thirteen colonies that made up our country. Great Britain was a **monarchy** ruled by a king. In a monarchy, a king or queen usually rules

their country for life before passing their power on to one of their children to take over.

Our Founding Fathers thought the kings and queens living in England had way too much power. So they created a set of rules for electing our leader: the president. They wrote these rules into the Constitution and its <u>AMENDMENTS</u>. In fact, the first words of the Constitution are

These are rules that were added to the Constitution later.

"We the people."

In other words, *we* (the people!) get to decide what's important and who's in charge of our country.

THE THREE BRANCHES OF GOVERNMENT

The president is just one little part of the US government. Our democracy is actually divided into three parts, or branches. Each branch has a different job. The three branches make up our <u>FEDERAL</u> government. That's the national government that makes rules for the entire country. **Each state has its own government, too!** And none of the branches—not even the president's—has total power.

The **EXECUTIVE BRANCH** *enforces the laws*. It's made up of the **president, vice president**, and their <u>CABINET</u>. The president lives and works in the **White House** and has many responsibilities. (We'll learn more about those on page 12.)

The **LEGISLATIVE BRANCH** *makes the laws* for the US people. It's run by **Congress**, which is made up of two parts: the **Senate** and the **House of Representatives**. Congress meets in the **US Capitol building**.

The **JUDICIAL BRANCH** *helps explain the laws* of our country and decides if laws have been broken. It's made up of **courts** and **judges**.

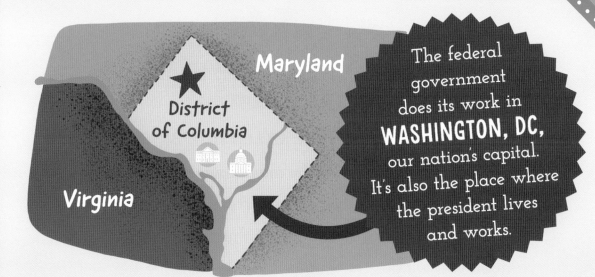

Maryland

District of Columbia

Virginia

The federal government does its work in **WASHINGTON, DC,** our nation's capital. It's also the place where the president lives and works.

THE SENATE

★ 100 members (two for each state)

★ We elect them every six years.

THE HOUSE OF REPRESENTATIVES

★ 435 members (The number of representatives from each state depends on the state's population. States with more people get more representatives.)

★ We elect them every two years.

The Speaker of the House is the head of the House of Representatives. After the vice president, they are the second in line to take over the office if something happens to the president.

THE SUPREME COURT is the highest court in the land. There are *nine justices* on the court, and they serve for their entire lives. (That's a long time!)

PRESENTING THE PRESIDENT

THE LEADER OF THE EXECUTIVE BRANCH

The US president is one of the most powerful people in the world. But they get their power from us—the American people who voted for them. And if the president doesn't do a good job, we get the chance to pick someone better the next time around.

The president's responsibilities include the following:

- Approving laws written by Congress. (The president can also choose to VETO a law, or not approve it.)
- Making sure the US people follow the approved laws.
- Choosing people for important jobs such as judges, ambassadors, and department heads.
- Commanding the branches of the US military.
- Meeting with leaders of other nations.
- Issuing executive orders, or rules. These are sometimes used to deal with emergencies or wars.

EXECUTIVE POWER

The actions a president takes while in office can change the nation for generations to come. Here are a few major **executive orders** issued by past presidents that had a big impact:

ABRAHAM LINCOLN issued the Emancipation Proclamation in 1863: an executive order that eventually ended slavery in the United States.

HARRY S. TRUMAN desegregated the US military through an executive order in 1948. This meant people of all races could finally serve side by side.

After the September 11, 2001, terrorist attacks, **GEORGE W. BUSH** signed an executive order to create the Department of Homeland Security. This department works to keep the United States safe from foreign threats.

WHO CAN VOTE?

The Constitution gives US citizens the right to vote in presidential elections. But babies can't vote—and neither can your pets! You must meet certain requirements before you can cast your ballot:

☑ **CITIZENSHIP** ☑

Voters must be US citizens. People who were born in the United States or in a US territory are citizens. People who move here from other countries can become citizens, too. They have to fill out an application, live in the country for a certain number of years, and pass a test about the United States.

☑ **AGE** ☑

If you are reading this, you might be too young to vote right now. You must be eighteen years old to vote in all US elections.

☑ **REGISTRATION** ☑

In most places, you can't just walk into the voting booth and say "It's showtime!" You must first register to vote in the state where you live. The rules, such as how long before an election you need to register, are different from state to state.

IT'S A FACT

In most parts of the United States, people in prison are not allowed to vote. However, in many states, when someone gets out of prison, they are allowed to vote again.

FIGHTING FOR YOUR RIGHT

Imagine you went into a time machine and zoomed back to the very first US presidential election. You'd notice something odd: Less than 1 percent of people actually voted in the first election in 1789. And pretty much all of them were wealthy white men.

Not everyone has always had the right to vote.

We sometimes call the right to vote "suffrage."

The US Constitution didn't include any rules about voting at first. So in the past, it was up to each state to make their own voting laws. And some groups were unfairly discriminated against.

But the Constitution is a "living" document. No, it doesn't *actually* have a heartbeat and a set of lungs, but we're able to change the Constitution by adding new amendments, or rules. Some of those rules have helped give more people the right to vote.

DEVOTED TO VOTING

While more groups have gained **SUFFRAGE** over time, these changes didn't just happen overnight—or without a fight. People **marched**, **protested**, and **spoke out** to get the right to vote. Standing up for what's right can really make a difference!

Keep reading to learn how voting rights in the United States have changed throughout history.

1800 | | | | 1850 | | | | 1900 | :

1789

Each state decides who can vote. The states only allow free white men who own property to vote.

1920

The **Nineteenth Amendment** grants women in all states the right to vote.

1870

The **Fifteenth Amendment** makes it against the law to stop someone from voting because of their race or color. Even so, people find ways to prevent Black citizens from voting. (Learn more about this on pages 64–67.)

WE DEMAND VOTING RIGHTS NOW!

VOTING RIGHTS NOW!

1965

The **Voting Rights Act** protects the right to vote for people of all races.

1924

Indigenous peoples gain US citizenship with the **Indian Citizenship Act**. This opens the door for Indigenous peoples to be able to vote.

OLD ENOUGH TO FIGHT, OLD ENOUGH TO VOTE!

1971

The **Twenty-Sixth Amendment** lowers the voting age from twenty-one to eighteen.

1950   2000

1943

Chinese immigrants get the right to citizenship and to vote.

1990

The **Americans with Disabilities Act** makes it illegal to discriminate against people with disabilities. This includes requiring government officials to make polling places and voting accessible to all.

VOTING IS PEOPLE POWER

UN-RESTRICTED VOTING RIGHTS!

I'M A VOTER

BLACK SUFFRAGE

Black people couldn't vote for many years. Then in 1870, the **Fifteenth Amendment** was passed, making it against the law to stop someone from voting because of their race or color. Even so, many Black people still faced great discrimination and were prevented from voting—at times with violence and intimidation. In 1965, Martin Luther King Jr. led a voting rights march in Alabama, and thousands

joined in protest. That same year, the **Voting Rights Act** was passed. It protects the right to vote for people of all races, finally forcing local authorities to follow the Fifteenth Amendment.

WOMEN'S SUFFRAGE

The Declaration of Independence says "all men are created equal"—and people took that literally for many years. Only men could vote in most states. But women across the country attended marches, wore buttons, and spoke out. In 1848, they gathered at a convention in Seneca Falls, New York, to talk about women's rights. In 1920, after nearly a hundred years of fighting, women in all states gained the right to vote with the enactment of the **Nineteenth Amendment**—though this mostly applied to white women. It would be years before many women of color would be able to vote.

LOWERING THE VOTING AGE

In the 1960s and 1970s, men as young as eighteen years old were drafted to fight in the Vietnam War. Many lost their lives. At the time, you had to be twenty-one years old to vote. But young people across the country protested. How could you be forced to fight for your country when you didn't even have a say in the war? Their voices were heard, and the protests led to the **Twenty-Sixth Amendment** in

1971. It lowered the voting age from twenty-one to eighteen. Some people think the voting age should be lowered even more, to sixteen. What do you think?

SO YOU WANT TO BE PRESIDENT?

The United States has often been called a place where any kid can grow up to be the president. That's basically true! The Constitution lists only three requirements to be president:

TO QUALIFY FOR THE JOB, YOU MUST . . .

- Be a citizen of the United States at birth;
- Be at least thirty-five years old; and
- Have lived in the United States for at least fourteen years.

Being the president of the United States is a huge job! But in many ways, it's like any other job out there. In addition to a job description (which you saw on page 12), it comes with a salary, coworkers, and some basic guidelines.

TIME IN OFFICE

Presidents serve four-year terms. A president can serve a maximum of two terms.

SALARY

The president makes $400,000 annually.

LOCATION

The president lives in and works from the White House in Washington, DC.

COWORKERS

Including members of the armed forces, more than four million Americans work under the president as part of the Executive Branch. The president also has a team of close advisors. (You'll learn more about them on pages 96–99).

IT'S A FACT

The president can only be elected twice. But this didn't become the law until 1951. Before that, **FRANKLIN D. ROOSEVELT** was elected president four times!

MANY PRESIDENTS COME FROM SIMILAR BACKGROUNDS

Of the first forty-six US presidents . . .

- All of them were men.

- All of them had at least one sibling.

- All but one of them were white. **BARACK OBAMA** was the first Black president.

- Thirty-one had served in the military.

- Twenty-seven had been lawyers.

- Nineteen had been in the US House of Representatives.

- Seventeen had been US senators.

IT'S A FACT

There have been forty-six US presidents—but only forty-five different people have served as president. How is that even possible? Well, **GROVER CLEVELAND** was president for two terms—but he didn't serve his two terms in a row. He was the twenty-second president, from 1885 to 1889, and then the twenty-fourth president, from 1893 to 1897.

GROVER CLEVELAND

DEMOCRATIC CANDIDATE

FOR PRESIDENT 1892

WHITE HOUSE

Grover Cleveland's SECOND presidential camapaign political ribbon

The **average age** of a president when they start the job is fifty-five years old. The **youngest** president was **THEODORE ROOSEVELT**. He became president at age forty-two. The **oldest** president elected was **JOE BIDEN**, who became president at age seventy-eight in 2021.

YOUNGEST

OLDEST

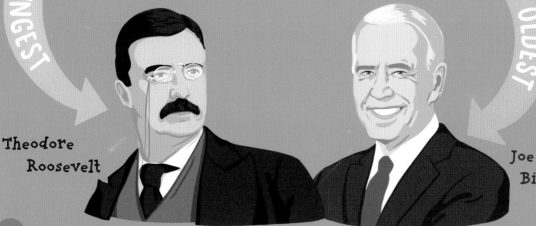

Theodore Roosevelt

Joe Biden

DID YOU KNOW THAT SOME OF THE PRESIDENTS HAVE BEEN RELATED TO EACH OTHER?

- JOHN ADAMS and JOHN QUINCY ADAMS were father and son. So were GEORGE H. W. BUSH and GEORGE W. BUSH.

- WILLIAM HENRY HARRISON and BENJAMIN HARRISON were grandfather and grandson.

George H. W. Bush (father) and George W. Bush (son)

- JAMES MADISON and ZACHARY TAYLOR were second cousins. And THEODORE ROOSEVELT and FRANKLIN D. ROOSEVELT were distant cousins.

William Henry Harrison (grandfather) and Benjamin Harrison (grandson)

★ RUNNING FOR PRESIDENT ★

THE LONG AND WINDING ROAD TO THE WHITE HOUSE

Running for president **STARTS** with an announcement. If you're lucky, it **ENDS** with a move into the White House. Follow along on the path below—just try not to get dizzy.

DEBATES!

Candidates from both parties argue about the important issues, such as health care, taxes, and the environment.

CAMPAIGNING BEGINS

Candidates travel the country giving speeches and talking to voters.

START

<u>CANDIDATES</u> announce their plans to run for president.

This often happens the spring or summer before an election year. Presidential elections take place in the United States every four years.

VOTE FOR CHANGE

THE NATIONAL CONVENTIONS

The Democrats and Republicans each pick one presidential candidate to put on the ballot.

This happens in late summer of an election year.

A **vice president is selected** to run with each presidential candidate.

MORE CAMPAIGNING

The top candidate for each party continues giving speeches and speaking with voters on the **CAMPAIGN** trail.

PRIMARIES and **CAUCUSES** take place.

This occurs during the spring and summer of an election year.

MORE DEBATES!

The Republican and Democratic candidates square off against each other in front of a national audience.

These debates take place the month before the presidential election.

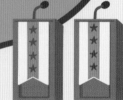

It's Election Day!

Voters head to the polls and pick the candidate they think will do the best job.

Election Day is in early November of an election year.

The president is picked.

Votes are counted and a winner is announced. Soon, a new president will take office—or a sitting president will serve their second term.

FINISH

IT'S (POLITICAL) PARTY TIME!

What's a <u>POLITICAL PARTY</u>**? Well, you don't have to bring a** gift and there won't be any cake. A political party is a group of people who feel the same way about many of the issues that are important to the country.

Political parties pick candidates to run for office, help organize the government, and raise money for candidates so they can run their election campaigns.

The people in a political party want someone in their own party to be elected to office. Here's the basic idea: If someone in your political party is elected, that person probably supports the same rules, laws, and changes you support. It's a win for the whole team!

The United States has what we call a *two-party system*. In other words, there are two major political parties: the **Democrats** and the **Republicans** Someone from one of these two parties has won every single presidential election since 1852.

DEMOCRATIC PARTY

SYMBOL: Donkey

COLOR: Blue

NICKNAME: The Dems

SOMETIMES CALLED:
Left Wing

YEAR FOUNDED: 1828

BELIEFS: Many Democrats are <u>LIBERAL</u>. They tend to think the government should use its power to fix things and help people.

REPUBLICAN PARTY

SYMBOL: Elephant

COLOR: Red

NICKNAME: The GOP
(this stands for "Grand Old Party")

SOMETIMES CALLED:
Right Wing

YEAR FOUNDED: 1854

BELIEFS: Many Republicans are <u>CONSERVATIVE</u>. They tend to think the government's power should be limited.

IT'S A FACT

Some candidates are **moderate**. That means they're not super liberal or super conservative. Instead, they fall somewhere in between—they think the government should have some power but not a ton. Both Democrats and Republicans can be moderates!

Although most US politicians and voters are either Democrats or Republicans, there are other political parties in the United States today. These parties are called **third parties**.

THE GREEN PARTY
cares about social justice, the planet, and protecting the environment for future generations.

THE LIBERTARIAN PARTY
believes that the government should pretty much stay out of people's lives and mind its own business.

Tired of political parties already? Politicians and voters can also decide to be INDEPENDENTS, or not be a member of any party.

PARTIES OF THE PAST

GEORGE WASHINGTON—the very first president!—was the only US president not in a political party. And some of the earliest presidents were members of political parties that no longer exist. After Washington came JOHN ADAMS. He was a member of the **Federalist Party**—the first political party in the United States. Federalists supported the Constitution and were in favor of a strong national government (as opposed to each individual state having more power).

★ ★ ★
SHOW YOUR PRIMARY COLORS

Almost anyone can run for president. And lots of people do! But before Election Day, the Republicans and the Democrats each need to pick just one candidate. They do this by holding events in each state called **primaries** and **caucuses**. These events generally take place from January through August of a presidential election year.

Think of primaries and caucuses as mini elections in each state. The voters in that state pick which Republican candidate and which Democratic candidate they want to run for president. If the current president has only had the job for four years, that person is almost *always* their party's candidate of choice for the next election.

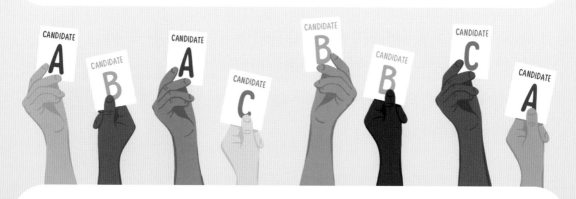

WHAT THE HECK IS A PRIMARY?

When choosing which candidate will represent each political party, most states hold primaries. Like most elections, primaries are done by a **secret vote**. In "open" primaries, voters can

> This means only you know which candidate you're voting for.

choose a candidate from any political party. For example, a Democrat could vote for a Republican candidate, or a Republican could vote for a Democrat. "Closed" primaries are a little bit different. You must choose a candidate from your own political party.

AND WHAT'S A CAUCUS?

Today, only a few states hold caucuses instead of primaries. **A caucus is like a series of meetings.** They happen in schools, town halls, and other gathering places across a state. Voters listen to speeches from their party's candidates and discuss their opinions. Then, they choose which candidate they think is best. In some cases, it's by a show of hands. Other times, voters break into groups to decide.

The Democrats and the Republicans do things a little differently. In most Republican caucuses, the candidate with the most votes wins. But in most Democratic caucuses, there are several rounds of voting. Candidates who get less than 15 percent of the vote are removed. Then the people who voted for them select another candidate. The process keeps going like this until they finally reach a winner.

A

B

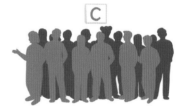
C

IT'S A FACT

All of the states originally held caucuses to pick the top candidates for president. But many states began switching to primaries in the early 1900s. People thought having party members vote directly for their top candidate was fairer.

STATES TO KEEP AN EYE ON

The first contest of a <u>NOMINATION</u> calendar takes place in January or February of an election year. **Being first is a big deal!** The results in these early caucuses and primaries can influence other states' decisions.

For years, the **Iowa caucus** came first for both Democrats and Republicans. But lately, the states have been battling it out to decide who gets to be first—or second or third! Some people want to give diverse voters more of a say in their party's pick for president, so they have bumped the contests in certain states up to earlier dates.

Keep an eye on **New Hampshire**, **South Carolina**, and **Nevada**.

These states hold some of the earliest primaries and caucuses in the country. The candidates who win these first few contests make a big splash. They become familiar faces and names to people in other states as their primaries and caucuses begin ramping up.

SUPER TUESDAY

EARLY PRIMARIES

Then in early March, there's **Super Tuesday**. It's a day when more than a dozen states hold their primaries and caucuses. More often than not, the winner of the majority of Super Tuesday states goes on to win their party's nomination. It's a pretty big day in the election cycle!

MARCH
S M T W Th F S

IT'S A FACT

Barack who? Many people thought **BARACK OBAMA** didn't stand a chance in the race until he won the Iowa Caucus in 2008. The big win in Iowa put Obama into the national spotlight—and he went on to become the forty-fourth president!

PICKING THE VICE PRESIDENT

We elect the president and vice president together, as a team. Before the big election, each presidential candidate picks the person they want to be their vice presidential running mate. It's ideally someone they'd partner well with!

Often, a candidate chooses a VP who will help **balance out the ticket**, or attract more types of voters. Perhaps they pick someone with a different viewpoint. Or maybe they choose someone of a different race, gender, age, or geographic location from them.

This wasn't always how the VP was selected. Until the early 1800s, the vice presidents were the candidates who got the second-most votes in a presidential election.

MADAME VICE PRESIDENT

President **JOE BIDEN** (who was the vice president from 2009 to 2017) picked **Kamala Harris** as his running mate during the 2020 presidential election. She became the first female vice president in US history. She was also the first Black person and first person of South Asian descent to hold the post.

vice president

JUST A HEARTBEAT AWAY

They say the vice president is just a heartbeat away from the presidency. That's because if anything ever happens to the president, **the VP is second-in-command** and must be ready to take over the job. This has actually happened a handful of times!

Fifteen vice presidents have gone on to be president. JOHN ADAMS was the nation's first vice president (under GEORGE WASHINGTON). He went on to be elected the second president of the United States.

Eight of these vice presidents took over after a president died in office. These presidents were all sworn in mid-term after the former president died or was killed:

JOHN TYLER, MILLARD FILLMORE, ANDREW JOHNSON, CHESTER A. ARTHUR, THEODORE ROOSEVELT, CALVIN COOLIDGE, HARRY S. TRUMAN, AND LYNDON B. JOHNSON.

One vice president took over after a president resigned. When RICHARD NIXON stepped down from office, GERALD FORD finished out the rest of the term as president.

IT'S A FACT

WILLIAM HENRY HARRISON was the first president to die in office—and the shortest-serving president in US history. (He was president for only thirty-one days before dying of pneumonia!) His VP, JOHN TYLER, took over as commander-in-chief and served out the rest of his term.

WILLIAM HENRY HARRISON FULL TERM						
	2	3	4	5	6	
7	8	9	10	11	12	13
14	15	16	17	18	19	20
21	22	23	24	25	26	27
28	29	30	★			

THE JOB DESCRIPTION

The vice president is more than just our nation's number two. For one, they're a top advisor to the president. The VP helps the president carry out their duties. They also travel around the world speaking to foreign leaders and make public appearances representing the president. It's a busy job!

The vice president is also the leader of the Senate. That means they cast the deciding vote in the Senate if there's a fifty-fifty tie.

★ DID YOU KNOW? ★

The vice president lives in a thirty-three-room house at the US Naval Observatory. It's just a short drive away from the White House.

The VP has an office in the West Wing of the White House.

The vice president's family is called the Second Family and the VP's spouse is known as the Second Lady or the Second Gentleman. Vice President Kamala Harris's husband, Douglas Emhoff, was the first-ever Second Gentleman.

IT'S A PARTY FOR YOUR PARTY!

Break out the disco balls and crank up the music: The <u>NATIONAL CONVENTIONS</u> are like a party for your party! After all the primaries and caucuses are over, each political party holds a big event in the late summer that's called—you guessed it!—a national convention. The conventions are held in a different US city every presidential election year. By the end of the conventions, the political parties have decided something huge: They've officially picked the person from their party who will be running for president.

WHO'S INVITED?

Every state and US territory sends people called <u>**DELEGATES**</u> to the national conventions. They are selected by the states during the primary and caucus contests. Each delegate has promised to support one of the party's presidential candidates.

ROLL CALL!

An important moment during a national convention is the roll call. **It's kind of like taking attendance in class.** The states are called in alphabetical order. A spokesperson from each state announces how many of that state's delegates are supporting each candidate.

TIME TO CELEBRATE

In the olden days, people didn't always know which candidate would be chosen at a party's national convention. Sometimes delegates supporting one candidate would try to get others to change their minds. They would have to do the roll call over and over (and over and over) again. Agreeing on one person wasn't an easy task!

Today, we usually know who the winners will be before the conventions even begin. During the primaries and caucuses, candidates keep track of how many **delegates** support them. If it's not enough to win at the convention, they often drop out of the presidential race. These candidates usually tell their delegates to support the leading candidate instead. Political parties like to be united behind one candidate. So these days, the roll-call vote is often unanimous—every delegate votes for the same person!

The celebration really begins on the last day of the convention. The person chosen to be their party's candidate gives an acceptance speech. Balloons and confetti drop from the ceiling and delegates wave colorful signs. Now it really looks like a party! But the hard work of winning over *even more* voters is about to start.

HOP ABOARD THE CAMPAIGN TRAIN

If you want to run for president, people need to know your name *and* they need a good reason to vote for you. That's where campaigning comes in. Campaigning is about spreading awareness for a candidate and convincing the American people that the candidate is the best person to do the job.

Campaigning is hard work! It starts the moment a candidate announces they are running for office—and it doesn't end until after Election Day.

Candidates travel all over the country, from state to state. They shake hands with voters, give speeches, and take selfies. They typically spend more time in states where the race is close so they can try to win over voters. These states are called <u>SWING STATES</u> or **battleground states**. (We'll learn more about those on page 82.)

Why are swing states so important? Well, in the United States, we have a special system for our presidential elections called the <u>ELECTORAL COLLEGE</u>. This means when candidates campaign, what they *really* need to do is win over the majority of voters in just a small number of these states where the race is anybody's game. (We'll talk more about the Electoral College beginning on page 77.)

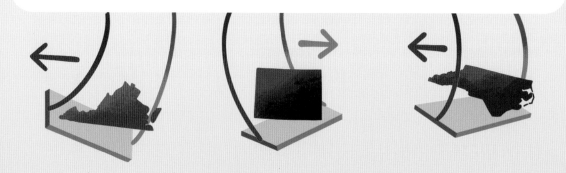

MEET THE TEAM

A lot of people work together to help a presidential campaign run smoothly. Here are just a few of the people who keep the campaign train running full steam ahead.

CAMPAIGN MANAGERS oversee the campaign and keep things organized.

SPEECHES
TRAVEL

VOTE for US

VOTE

CAMPAIGN STRATEGISTS come up with a game plan for winning.

COMMUNICATIONS DIRECTORS deal with the press and social media.

SPEECHWRITERS write speeches and brainstorm talking points for their candidate.

VOLUNTEERS make phone calls, pass out fliers, and go knocking door to door. They speak to everyday citizens (like you!) about the candidate they want to win. Some volunteers help get people out to vote on Election Day. Anybody can be a volunteer for their favorite candidate's campaign—including you (with the help of a grown-up)!

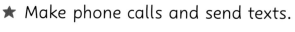
WAYS YOU CAN VOLUNTEER . . .

★ Make phone calls and send texts.

★ Knock on doors.

★ Put up posters or fliers.

★ Send letters.

★ Talk to your friends and family.

★ Host or attend a fundraiser.

GETTING THE WORD OUT

During election season, you'll see campaign messages just about everywhere. Signs on front lawns. Posters in windows. Bumper stickers on cars. T-shirts, hats, and buttons. Fliers, pamphlets, and mailed letters. Posts all over social media.

Many candidates come up with catchy **campaign slogans** to help them stick in voters' minds.

HERE ARE JUST A FEW OF THE MOST MEMORABLE CAMPAIGN SLOGANS PRESIDENTS HAVE USED OVER THE YEARS

THE LOG CABIN CANDIDATE
Wm. H. HARRISON
TIPPECANOE & TYLER TOO

William Henry Harrison (1840)

WIN WITH WILSON

Woodrow Wilson (1912)

KEEP COOL WITH COOLIDGE

Calvin Coolidge (1924)

WHO BUT HOOVER

Herbert Hoover (1928)

HAPPY DAYS ARE HERE AGAIN

Franklin D. Roosevelt (1932)

ALL THE WAY WITH LBJ 1964

Lyndon B. Johnson (1964)

MAKE AMERICA GREAT AGAIN

Donald Trump (2016)

ADVERTISEMENTS

Candidates advertise on television, radio, and online. Ads might include catchy tunes or promises to voters. Often, they tug at people's heartstrings and make voters feel hopeful for the future. But some candidates use ads to say negative things about their opponents instead.

ENDORSEMENTS

Famous people, including other politicians, sometimes publicly announce who they're voting for. Newspapers also sometimes announce which candidate they're supporting. These endorsements can really sway **undecided voters!**

Those are voters who haven't made up their mind yet.

IN THE NEWS

This just in! During election season, presidential candidates are all over the news. TV news stations feature **pundits** who give commentary about the candidates. This helps viewers form opinions.

Those are political experts!

Newspapers and online news sites also give the candidates press coverage. Reporters follow the candidates on the campaign trail and write about the facts. If a candidate behaves poorly, they inform people of the truth.

Newspaper Times

CANDIDATE Pulls Ahead in Big Race

"I'M DONKEY DEMOCRAT, AND I APPROVE THIS MESSAGE."

You'll hear similar words at the end of **all** political ads. It's actually the law! Since 2002, candidates running for federal office have been required to identify themselves and say that they approve of the messages in their advertisements. Lawmakers hoped this would cut down on negative ads.

"I APPROVE THIS MESSAGE."

WHERE DO I STAND?

Candidates sometimes have an idea of how they're doing in a race before Election Day. They rely on **POLLS**, or surveys of voters. A poll asks a random group of people who they plan to vote for. The idea is that the choices of the small group reflect the choices of a larger group of voters.

But polling isn't always correct, and **anything can happen on Election Day**. So even if the polls say that your favorite candidate is ahead by a lot, it's still important to go out and vote!

SHOW ME THE MONEY

Candidates don't have much hope of winning an election without the big bucks. They need money to pay for advertisements, travel, and more. They also need money to pay the many people who work for them throughout their campaign.

Candidates can get some money from the government to help pay for campaigning. But it's not really enough to make a big splash. Candidates need to raise even more money from donors, too.

Every donation helps. If you like a candidate, you can support them by donating a few dollars to their campaign. **Small donations from a lot of people really add up!**

Wealthy people sometimes like to donate a lot of money to their favorite candidates. But there's a limit to how much someone can give to one campaign. This makes it so that no person has too much power over what a candidate says or does.

Yet people can get around the donation limit by giving money to political action committees known as **PACs** and **Super PACs**. Those are political groups. People donate a lot of money to them, and in turn, they donate that money to political candidates.

CANDIDATE

IT'S A FACT

The 2020 elections were the most expensive in history. The presidential candidates spent over $5.7 billion on their campaigns. That's more than twice as much as the previous election cycle. JOE BIDEN raised over $1 billion from donors, more than any candidate in history.

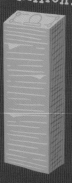

1 billion!

THE GREAT DEBATES

Kick up your feet and grab the popcorn—the *presidential debates* are not to be missed. In the weeks leading up to the election, the top Republican and Democratic candidates square off against each other. They take turns answering the same questions. Those running for president usually have three debates, and the vice-presidential candidates usually have one.

The debates are broadcast live on television, the radio, and the internet. Millions of citizens tune in . . . and you should, too!

Debates give people the chance to hear the candidates' opinions on many important topics. And they help undecided voters make the big decision of who to pick for president.

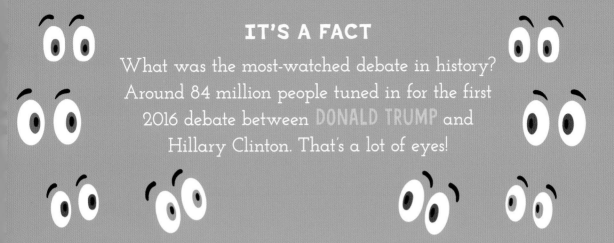

IT'S A FACT

What was the most-watched debate in history?
Around 84 million people tuned in for the first
2016 debate between DONALD TRUMP and
Hillary Clinton. That's a lot of eyes!

Tune in to watch the debates and you'll notice there's a lot going on. Each candidate stands up on a stage behind a podium. They talk into microphones and argue back and forth. Sometimes, the candidates get really passionate about certain issues and ideas. Watch and listen closely—you'll learn a lot about each candidate!

HERE'S WHAT YOU NEED TO KNOW
TO FOLLOW ALONG:

A **moderator** asks the questions and keeps things on track. Although sometimes audience members—even kids!—get to ask the candidates questions, too.

The **questions** at a debate can be tough! You might hear things like "What steps should be taken to address climate change?" or "What policies should be put in place to give all kids an equal opportunity to succeed?"

The candidates **take turns** answering the moderator's questions. The first candidate gets two minutes to answer. Then their opponent gets one minute to speak about the same topic. In the end, each candidate gives a two-minute **closing argument**.

The debates can get a little awkward. You might hear **interruptions** and **personal attacks**. Candidates on both sides sometimes raise their voices or call each other mean names. It's the moderator's job to keep everyone in line—which isn't always an easy task!

WHO WINS?

Who "wins" a presidential debate? That question is often up for debate! But here are a few things to look out for:

Do the candidates actually answer the question that's asked, or do they ramble on about other topics?

How do the candidates treat the moderator? Are they composed and polite?

Do the candidates stand their ground during stressful moments or lose their cool?

Which candidate does a better job at clearly explaining their ideas? (And whose ideas do you agree with?)

How well do the candidates sway voters who are on the fence?

FACT-CHECK!

Not everything the candidates say on the campaign trail is actually true. Sometimes, the candidates tell big and small lies to try to win over voters. It's important to not assume that everything you hear is a fact. Do your research. **Misinformation can be harmful!** Some news organizations even fact-check the debates in real time, and it can be helpful to follow along.

A HISTORIC DEBATE

The first debate that ever aired on TV was between RICHARD NIXON and **JOHN F. KENNEDY** in 1960. Kennedy looked young and healthy, but Nixon looked sweaty and nervous. Those who watched the debate on TV thought Kennedy did a better job. Some think his confident performance led to his victory in that year's race.

Richard Nixon

John F. Kennedy

One great thing about our democracy is that you're allowed to have your own views about the many issues people care about—*and* you're allowed to express your opinions about them. During elections, the candidates take a stance on some of these common issues.

THE ECONOMY

Candidates have opinions on how the United States should make and spend money and create new jobs. Some think the government should do more to help the economy, and others think the economy does better when the government stays out.

TAXES

Every US citizen pays taxes. The money helps pay for things like roads, schools, and parks. Even the president's paycheck comes from taxes! Presidential candidates usually have different opinions about whether taxes should be lower or higher.

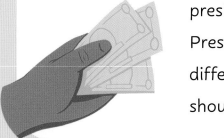

EDUCATION

Most candidates think every citizen deserves a good education. But many have different ideas of what that looks  like. For example, some think teachers need more training, and some argue that education should be more affordable.

HEALTH CARE

What happens when you get sick or hurt? Many citizens have insurance to help pay for their health care. Some candidates think the government should help pay for more of these costs.

FOREIGN RELATIONS

Should we go to war to help another country stay safe?  Some candidates say yes—fighting for other countries is the right thing to do, and it helps keep the United States powerful. Others think we should focus more on our own country.

CLIMATE

Some candidates think climate change is a major issue. They want to do more to protect the planet for future generations. Others think Earth isn't in such bad shape. They think doing things to help the environment could hurt businesses.

IMMIGRATION

Many people have immigrated to the United States from other countries. Some people think there are too many immigrants, and jobs and government money should go to US citizens. Others believe immigrants work hard and deserve a chance, too.

TIP

Is there an issue that *really* matters to you? Even if you're not old enough to vote, you can still let your voice be heard! **Write a letter** to a candidate expressing your opinion on the issue. Tell them what you think they should do about it. You might even get a letter back from a future president!

HOW DO YOU PICK WHO TO VOTE FOR?

You've seen the commercials and heard the campaign slogans. You've watched the candidates debate the issues of the day. Election Day is almost here, but now comes the hard part: **How on earth do you pick who to vote for?**

DECIDE WHICH ISSUES MATTER MOST TO YOU. Do you care more about taxes or the environment? Health care or education? You might choose to support the candidate who cares about the same issues you do.

LEARN MORE ABOUT THE POLITICAL PARTIES. You'll find a group of people who (mostly) agree with you on how the government should be run. If you're aligned with a political party, you'll likely support that party's candidate for president, too.

TALK (AND LISTEN!) TO OTHERS. It's a smart idea to chat with people who both agree and disagree with your opinions. This helps you better understand the country and where other people are coming from. Healthy and respectful debate is a good thing! And listening to others could help you form your own opinions about what matters.

FIGURE OUT IF A CANDIDATE KEEPS THEIR PROMISES. This might take a bit of research. If a candidate is running for a second term, investigate whether they actually did the things they said they would do in their first term. Do you want to give them a second chance, or vote for someone new?

★ GET OUT THE VOTE ★

IT'S ELECTION DAY!

There's a buzz in the air. People are walking with pep in their step. Everything could change—or things could stay mostly the same. But one thing's certain: The fate of the country rests in the hands of the American people. That's because it's Election Day, and every vote matters!

 ## Election Day is held on the Tuesday after the first Monday in November.

There's a good reason for this. In the past, many voters were farmers. They had to travel miles and miles to vote. Many went to church on Sundays and to the market to sell food on Wednesdays. So Tuesday was the best day of the week to hold elections.

November was after the busy harvest season had ended but before it got too cold outside—the perfect time to show up and vote!

VOTING WAY BACK WHEN

Voting in some of the first US presidential elections looked quite different than it does today. In the past, Election Day was a big public affair with parades, bands, banners, and floats. Back then, voting for president wasn't done in private like it is today. Instead, people voted by calling out the name of their chosen candidate.

This was called *viva voce*, or voice voting. Voters first had to swear on a Bible that they hadn't already cast a vote. Then, the voter called out his chosen candidate to a clerk. Yes, *his* chosen candidate. Remember: Women (and many other groups!) had to wait years to get the right to vote.

There were some other forms of voting back then, too. Sometimes, people voted by hand or by foot. They might stand on one side of a town hall if they supported one candidate and another side if they supported a different one. Or they'd stand or raise their hand in the air to show support for a candidate.

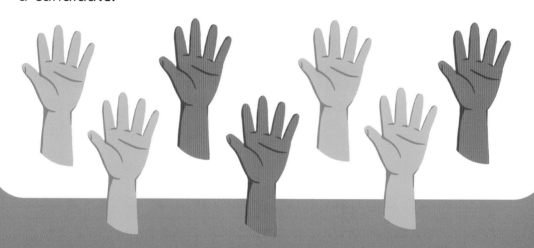

Voting may look different today, but it's still a day of great celebration. After all, voting means you're a part of this **cool** and **awesome** thing we call democracy. You have the power to shape the world for future generations!

SHOW UP AND VOTE!

It's so important to show up and vote on Election Day. A high **voter turnout** means more voices are heard. And when more people show up, our elected officials better represent the things the American people want and care about.

These days, more than 100 million people across the country will vote in a presidential election. That sounds like a lot of voters, but really, it's only around 60 percent of people who are old enough to vote.

Here in the United States, you have to **register to vote** before you can participate in an election. How exactly do you register to vote? Well, that depends on the state you live in. Some places register people automatically when they get a driver's license. Others allow voters to register at their polling place on Election Day when they show up to cast their ballots. And in some places, you can register online.

Look up how voter registration works in your own state! Then encourage the grown-ups in your life to check their voter registration status.

IT'S A FACT

Voting is actually required by law in some countries. For example, if you don't vote in Australia, you have to pay a fine. Some people argue the United States should also require all citizens to vote. What do you think?

★ ★ ★ SUPPRESSING THE VOTE

Voting is *so* important, but some people care more about winning elections than they do about fairness and democracy. Over the years, **many states have worked to deny certain groups of people the right to vote.** People still found ways to discriminate against Black voters and other people of color, despite the many laws and Constitutional amendments passed to give more Americans the right to vote. These people thought the only way of winning an election was to be sneaky and to keep people likely to vote for their opponent from voting at all. That goes against everything our democracy stands for! Here are just a few ways voter suppression has been used to prevent eligible people from voting.

UNTIL 1915 . . .

There was a **grandfather clause**. The clause said that if your grandfather didn't vote, you couldn't vote, either. The grandfather clause was unfair to Black voters, because most of their grandparents *couldn't* vote because they had been enslaved. The grandfather clause prevented almost all Black people at the time from voting.

UNTIL 1964 . . .

Poll taxes in most Southern states prevented many Black people from voting. In order to register to vote, you were required to first pay a fee. Many people couldn't afford the fee, so they didn't get the chance to make their voices heard.

UNTIL 1965 . . .

Many people of color in the South had to take a **literacy test** before they could register to vote. These tests targeted Black voters and were designed to be impossible to pass. They asked questions about laws and logic—and some had more than thirty questions! The person giving the test got to decide whether to ask easy or hard ones. If you failed the test, you couldn't vote!

VOTER SUPPRESSION TODAY

We've made a lot of progress over the years, but **voter suppression still exists today**. In some states, voters are required to show a photo ID at the polls. If they don't have an ID, they're turned away and can't vote. Getting an ID (like a driver's license) takes time and costs money. Not everybody is able to get one. In fact, this requirement

hits people of color the hardest. It also impacts low-income and elderly communities.

Other voters are discriminated against when their polling places close down. More than a thousand polling places in the American South have closed in the past decade. This is especially hard on Black and brown voters, disabled voters, and those from lower-income families. Fewer polling places means people have to travel farther and wait in longer lines in order to vote. In the 2016 election, smartphone data showed that Black voters across the country had to wait in longer lines than white voters. In Georgia, it's even against the law to bring food or water to people waiting in long lines to vote.

These tactics really discourage voters! They are often done by people of one political party who want to keep voters from the opposite party away from the polls.

THE COLD HARD TRUTH ABOUT GERRYMANDERING

Long lines and unfair policies aren't the only reasons voters stay home on Election Day. Some people think that their vote doesn't really count. This can be the case in a state or district affected by <u>GERRYMANDERING</u>.

Gerry WHAT? Each state is divided into election districts. Politicians pick and draw the districts' boundaries, or edges. **Sometimes, the districts are drawn in an unfair way to help one political party over another.** This is known as gerrymandering.

Say you have a state voting on whether to eat pizza or sandwiches for lunch. There's a "pizza party" and a "sandwich party."

The sandwich party might draw the district boundaries in a way that spreads the pizza party out across many different districts. If they're all spread out, it's hard for the pizza party to get a majority of votes. Or the sandwich party could pack as many pizza voters as possible into just a few districts. That way, pizza would get the majority of votes in only a few places, giving sandwiches the advantage.

SANDWICH PARTY GERRYMANDER

Divided pizza votes

Sandwich Wins ● ● ● ●   Pizza Wins ● ● ●

Limited pizza districts

Sandwich Wins ● ● ● ●   Pizza Wins ● ●

Gerrymandering isn't very fair—but both Republicans and Democrats do it. A political party in power might draw their state's districts in a way that helps their own party win in future elections.

Gerrymandering discourages voters and can lead to lower voter turnout. But it's important to remember that every single vote counts, no matter where you live or which political party is in power.

IT'S A FACT

The term gerrymander comes from a politician named Elbridge Gerry. In 1812, he approved of a bill to draw new districts for the state of Massachusetts. One redrawn district looked like a salamander! We still use the term today to describe the process of drawing new, funny-shaped districts.

BEHOLD THE BALLOT

If you're voting in person on Election Day, you go to a polling place. Polling places are often in schools, libraries, community centers, or other common spots near where you live.

There are several different ways to cast your vote. Some places have **voting machines**. You make your selections on a computer screen by pressing buttons or using a touch screen. But many places use **paper ballots**.

The ballots can be full of things to vote for. In addition to national candidates (like the president!), you might vote for state or local candidates, school board members, or local laws.

¿No hablas ingles? No te preocupes. Ballots come in several languages. And every voter has the right to translation or bilingual assistance when voting.

HE VOTADO HOY

Filling in a paper ballot is easy. Grab a pen with blue or black ink. Then fill in the circle next to the candidates and issues you want to vote for.

Not happy with any of your options? There's a blank spot on the ballot for a **write-in candidate**. In other words, you can write the name of someone, *anyone*, you'd like to vote for here. However, it's very (very!) unlikely that candidate would actually win.

You can only vote one time in an election. Voting more than once is called **VOTER FRAUD**, and it's a crime! Don't worry though: Voter fraud isn't very common in US elections.

★★★ OTHER WAYS TO VOTE

Not everybody votes in person—and not everybody votes on Election Day, either. Some states allow **early voting**. You can show up and vote in person on select dates before the big day. People with busy work schedules sometimes prefer to vote this way.

But what happens if you can't make it to the polls on Election Day *or* during early voting? Maybe you're out of town, sick, or serving in the military. Don't worry—you can still vote! With **ABSENTEE VOTING** and **mail-in voting**, you can cast a vote by mail before the election takes place. That's right: You can vote from the comfort of your home!

Here's how it works: A ballot is sent to your address. You fill it out and send it back in the mail before the deadline. In some places, you can drop it off in a secure ballot drop-off box or bring it to your local elections office instead.

A record number of people voted early and by mail in the 2020 presidential election. The election took place during the coronavirus pandemic, and people were worried about getting sick if they showed up to vote in person on Election Day.

These days, many people still prefer to vote by mail. You don't have to brave long Election Day lines, and you can take your time at home researching the candidates and the issues. How do you think you'll cast your first ballot?

IT'S A FACT

What about the astronauts who are up in space on Election Day? Astronauts who are US citizens use a special process to vote. They securely email their choices on the ballot back down to Earth. Talk about out-of-this-world voting!

A PEEK INSIDE THE POLLING PLACE

Welcome to your local polling place. Take a look around!

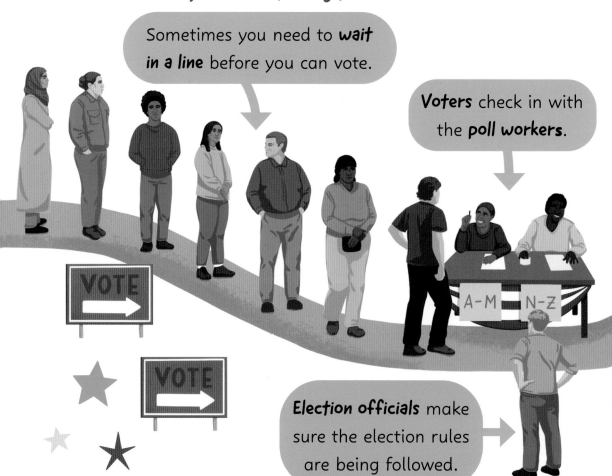

Sometimes you need to **wait in a line** before you can vote.

Voters check in with the **poll workers**.

VOTE

VOTE

A-M   N-Z

Election officials make sure the election rules are being followed.

IT'S A FACT

You're not allowed to campaign at or near a polling place on Election Day. That means no signs, no fliers, and no T-shirts or hats promoting the candidates. You're not even allowed to try to convince someone there who to vote for. It's against the law!

When it's your turn to vote, you might go into a **voting booth**. The presidential election uses a **secret ballot**. This means nobody else can see who you voted for. But there's an exception: Most kids are allowed in the voting booth with their parents!

VOTE COUNTED

BALLOT

You place your ballot in a **ballot box** or feed it into a **machine**.

Hurray! Grab an "I Voted" sticker— you did it!

Many ballots are counted automatically by a machine. It scans and counts each vote. But some paper ballots need to be counted by hand, one by one.

I VOTED

★ AND THE NEXT PRESIDENT IS... ★

THE VOTES POUR IN

In the eastern United States, polls begin closing at six o'clock at night. The final polls close seven hours later in western Alaska. If a voter is in line before the polls close, they still get to vote. In some places, the lines can be very long. But voters wait patiently for their chance to have a say.

On election night, people across the nation turn on their televisions, log onto social media, and hit refresh on websites as the vote counts pour in. News stations have live coverage of the election all night long.

Once the polls close in a state, a winner is projected for that state—unless the race is very close. Sometimes we know who the next president will be on election night. But if it's a nail-biter, it can take days for the winner to be announced.

RESULTS ROLL IN

185   173

THE ELECTORAL COLLEGE

Election Day is over! Now the candidate who got the most votes across the country wins, right? Well, not always. And it isn't that simple, either. That's because the United States has something called the **Electoral College**. It has nothing to do with a college where people go to learn. In fact, the Electoral College isn't even a place!

The Founding Fathers came up with the idea. They couldn't decide if the president should be elected by Congress or by a **POPULAR VOTE** of citizens. They also didn't want the states where the fewest people live to be ignored in the presidential election. The Electoral College was their compromise. With the electoral system, every state—big or small—gets a say.

The Electoral College can be a bit confusing—but it's an important thing to understand if you want to follow along on Election Day!

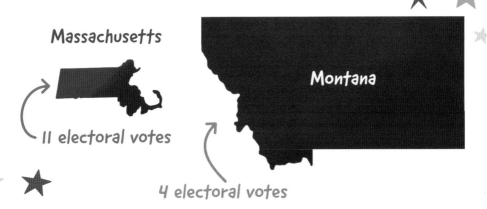

Massachusetts

11 electoral votes

Montana

4 electoral votes

Here's how the Electoral College works: Each state gets a certain number of <u>ELECTORS</u>—**one for each senator** (that's two per state) and **one for each US representative** (that number is different per state and depends on the state's population). Oh, and then there are also **three electors for Washington, DC**. (Our nation's capital isn't actually a part of any state—but its citizens still get a say in presidential elections!)

100 SENATORS

+ **435** MEMBERS OF THE HOUSE OF REPRESENTATIVES

+ **3** VOTES FOR WASHINGTON, D.C.

538 TOTAL VOTES

So in total, there are **538 members** of the Electoral College. To win the presidency, a candidate needs at least **270 electoral votes**. That's one more than half of the total electoral votes. (Talk about a lot of math!)

Don't forget: The number of electoral votes each state has depends on **population size**, not the size of the state itself. A smaller state like New Jersey has a lot of people living in it, so it has fourteen electoral votes. A bigger state like New Mexico has fewer people living there, so it gets only five.

DID YOU KNOW?

The number of electoral votes each state gets can change every ten years. Florida had only four electoral votes in the Electoral College in 1900. Then in 1964, it had fourteen electoral votes. And for the 2024 election, it was up to thirty electoral votes. How is that even possible? Well, Florida's population has grown over time. Over the years, the state has been given more electoral votes to better reflect the number of people living there. This means it's more important for a candidate to win Florida today than it was in the past. It's worth a lot of votes—and it's also a place where the presidential race can be anybody's game. (That makes Florida a **swing state**—you'll learn more about those on page 82.)

States can also lose electoral votes if their population decreases.

IT'S A FACT

RONALD REAGAN got the highest number of electoral votes of any president, winning 525 of the total 538 in 1984.

Did you know that when you vote for president, you're not directly voting for a candidate? You're really telling the electors in your state to vote for the candidate you like. **If a candidate wins the most votes in a state, they get all of that state's electoral votes.***

Maine and Nebraska do things differently. They sometimes split their electoral votes! In these states, the winners of each district get one electoral vote. And the person who wins the state's popular vote gets two.

Let's look at Missouri for example. The Show-Me State had ten electoral votes as of 2024. So before Election Day, both the Republicans and the Democrats pick ten people to be their electors. If the majority of people in Missouri vote for the Republican candidate, they get all ten Republican electoral votes. If the majority of people in Missouri vote for the Democrat, that candidate gets all ten votes from the Democratic electors. (The losing party's electors don't get to vote.)

Remember, to win the race you need **270 electoral votes**. The candidates usually want to focus their energy on states where the race is closer and either candidate has a chance of winning. Winning a state with ten votes here and a state with twelve votes there can really add up!

BLUE STATES, RED STATES, AND PURPLE STATES

If you watch the results pour in on election night, you'll see a big Electoral College map full of blue and red states. **Many states have supported the same political party in pretty much every recent presidential election.**

BLUE STATES

These states usually support the Democratic candidate. They're often found on the West Coast and in the Northeast. (California's a blue state.)

RED STATES

These states usually support the Republican candidate. They're generally found in the Southern and central parts of the country. (Alabama's a red state.)

But some states go back and forth depending on the year, candidate, or election. These are called **swing states**, or **battleground states**. These states are usually less predictable. Some years, swing states select the Republican candidate. Other years, they go for the Democrat. (That's why they're sometimes called PURPLE STATES—they're a combination of red and blue!)

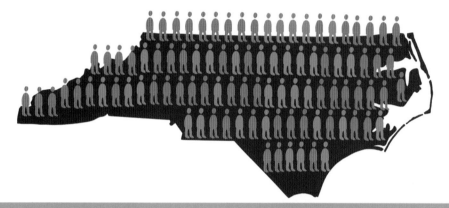

Candidates spend a lot of time campaigning in swing states to try to win over voters. After all, if an election is close, it's probably decided by a small number of key swing states. It's true the battleground states are worth fewer electoral votes than states like California and Texas. But winning them is often crucial to getting the 270 electoral votes needed to win the presidency.

ELECTION SHOCKS AND SURPRISES

Some years, a presidential election goes pretty much according to plan. The candidate who seems to be ahead in the race wins the election and becomes the next president. But this isn't always how a presidential election goes down. There have been years when things got a little more complicated.

WHAT IF NO ONE WINS A MAJORITY?

Say neither candidate gets the 270 electoral votes they need to win. How do we figure out who becomes the president then? If this happens, **the next president is picked by the House of Representatives**. Each state gets one vote. The representatives from each state get together and decide who they will pick. Whichever candidate gets at least **twenty-six votes** (one more than half of the fifty total states) wins.

The presidential election of 1824 was decided by the House of Representatives. **ANDREW JACKSON** ran against **JOHN QUINCY ADAMS**. Neither candidate got a majority of electoral votes, so it was up to the House of Representatives to make the final decision. Although Andrew Jackson won the popular vote, the House picked John Quincy Adams to be the nation's sixth president.

IT'S A FACT

The United States developed a *two-party system* because of the Electoral College. Having more political parties would split up the vote too much and make it harder for any candidate to win 270 electoral votes—and the presidency.

LOSING THE POPULAR VOTE

Most of the time, the candidate who wins the most overall votes in the country gets the most electoral votes, too. But as you just read, this wasn't the case with **ANDREW JACKSON**. And it hasn't been the case with four other presidential candidates, either.

The five candidates shown here won the popular vote but not the electoral vote. In other words, most of the United States voted for them—but because of the Electoral College system, they didn't get to be the next president.

Andrew Jackson in 1824
(lost to John Quincy Adams)

Samuel J. Tilden in 1878
(lost to Rutherford B. Hayes)

Grover Cleveland in 1888
(lost to Benjamin Harrison)

Al Gore in 2000
(lost to George W. Bush)

Hillary Clinton in 2016
(lost to Donald Trump)

IT'S A FACT

Not everyone is in favor of the Electoral College. In fact, there have been more than **seven hundred proposals** to change or get rid of it. Some people think the candidate who wins the popular vote *should* win the election, no matter what. What do you think?

TOO CLOSE TO CALL?

Sometimes, an election is very, very close. And there have been times when people have doubts about the election results, too. They think the ballots weren't all properly counted. If this happens, a state might have to recount all the votes. This can take a lot of time! And it's happened more than once in the last few decades.

GEORGE W. BUSH vs. AL GORE (2000)

The vote total in Florida was super close, so a recount began. It took over a month to declare **GEORGE W. BUSH** the forty-third president.

FL

JOE BIDEN VS. DONALD TRUMP (2020)

Counties in several battleground states recounted ballots after close votes. It took four days for **JOE BIDEN** to be declared the projected winner.

News organizations are often eager to be the first to declare a winner in a presidential election—but if they guess the results too soon, they can announce the wrong person! This happened in the 1948 presidential election between Thomas Dewey and **HARRY S. TRUMAN**. It seemed like Dewey was ahead in the race.

In fact, the morning after the election, the *Chicago Daily Tribune* printed a big headline on the front page that read "Dewey Defeats Truman." Dewey, however, never made it to the White House—Truman was the actual winner. There's a famous photo of Truman, the PRESIDENT-ELECT, holding a copy of the incorrect newspaper with a huge smile.

That's what we call the person who has won the election but has not yet been sworn in.

GOOD WINNERS AND LOSERS

Once the American people have had their say, a new president is picked to lead the nation. Whether a candidate wins or loses, they've accomplished something great—and they can begin looking to the future.

Losing is never fun, but the way a candidate behaves when they lose an election really matters. Candidates trust the election process and respect the will of the American people. After all, they can always run again in the future. But this time around, the American people picked someone else, so it's their time to step down.

Candidates know it's important to be a good sport. After the projected winner is announced, the losing candidate **concedes**, or announces their defeat. They give a speech thanking their voters for believing in them. They call and congratulate the winner on their victory. If a president in office doesn't get elected for a second term, they prepare to leave the office when their term is up.

This is called the **peaceful transfer of power**. Leaving the top office with grace is an important part of our elections. It's what makes our democracy work!

THE GREAT TRANSITION

There are about eleven weeks between Election Day and INAUGURATION Day. It's a time of big transition—where not much else gets done at the White House. After all, the president no longer has much power.

This time period actually has a name! It's called the LAME-DUCK PERIOD. The president uses this time to get the president-elect up to speed.

Meanwhile, the incoming First Family picks out furniture they like for the White House, plus their favorite snacks, bath soaps, and more. (But they won't actually move into the White House until Inauguration Day!)

When a president leaves office, they often leave a note of advice and encouragement for the person taking over.

Ronald Reagan's letter to George H. W. Bush (1989)

Don't let the turkeys get you down.

Dear George
You'll have moments when you want to use this particular stationery. Well, go to it.
George I treasure the memorys we share and wish you all the very best. You'll be in my prayers. God Bless you & Barbara. I'll miss our Thursday lunches.
Ron

IT'S A FACT

The lame-duck period used to be pretty long. In the past, it lasted from November to March! But it was officially shortened in 1933 when the Twentieth Amendment went into effect.

LET'S GET INAUGURATED!

The presidential inauguration usually takes place January 20 following the election in November. It's a pretty exciting day! The president-elect officially becomes the president when they are sworn into office. People eat, dance, and celebrate late into the night. If a sitting president is elected to serve a second term, their second inauguration is usually less of a big deal—but it's still a day worth celebrating. Here's how the big day usually unfolds:

1. TO THE CAPITOL
The current president and president-elect travel together from the White House to the Capitol building.

2. THE VICE PRESIDENT
On the inaugural platform, the VP-elect takes the oath of office. They repeat a promise to follow the rules of, and defend, the US Constitution.

3. THE PRESIDENT
At noon, the president-elect officially becomes the new president by taking the oath of office.

4. INAUGURAL ADDRESS
The president gives a speech and talks about their goals for leading the country.

IT'S A FACT

WiLLiAM HENRY HARRiSON gave *the longest* presidential inauguration speech in history. It was one hour and 45 minutes long—and he gave it in the pouring rain!

GEORGE WASHINGTON's second inaugural address was *the shortest* in history—just 135 words.

5. LUNCHTIME
After the speech, the new president goes inside the US Capitol for the inaugural luncheon.

6. THE PRESIDENTiAL PARADE
The president and vice president lead a parade with marching bands, floats, and a huge cheering crowd!

7. PARTY TiME
At night, it's time for the inaugural balls: big, fancy parties to celebrate the president.

★ LIFE IN THE WHITE HOUSE ★

★★★ THE PRESIDENT HARD AT WORK

Finally, after the inauguration in late January, the hard work of being president of the United States begins. The president has many duties (you can read about them on pages 12–13), and the American people are watching them very closely. In fact, their **first one hundred days** in office are key. In these first few months, it becomes clear how successful the president will be at getting things done.

During the day, you can find the president hard at work in the **Oval Office**. It's exactly what it sounds like: an office in the shape of an oval. It's in the **West Wing** of the White House (where the president lives), so it doesn't take the president very long to get to work.

But the president also spends a lot of time on the go. They travel around the country—and the world!—in a private jet called **Air Force One**. The president meets with foreign leaders, visits natural disaster sites, and gives speeches.

Among the president's many speaking duties is giving the annual **State of the Union address** to the American people. Citizens everywhere tune in to hear the president talk about issues facing the country and the president's ideas on how to fix things.

If you want to be the president, you have to be good at keeping secrets. Presidents have the power of **executive privilege**, which means they keep some matters secret in order to make the best possible decisions and help keep people safe.

Speaking of all things secret: Being the president can be a dangerous job. That's where the **Secret Service** comes in. The Secret Service protects the president and their family from any threats. There's at least one secret service member with the president at all times (even in the bathroom!).

IT'S A FACT

Presidents are given secret service code names like *Searchlight* (**RICHARD NIXON**), *Timberwolf* (**GEORGE H. W. BUSH**), and *Celtic* (**JOE BIDEN**). Even VPs and members of the First Family get secret service code names. **BARACK OBAMA'S** two daughters, Malia and Sasha, had the code names *Radiance* and *Rosebud*.

THE FIRST LADY (OR FIRST GENTLEMAN)

If the president has a female partner, this woman is known as the First Lady. She doesn't just sit back and let the president do all the important stuff. **The First Lady plays an important role in the affairs of the country.** She even has an office in the White House!

The First Lady isn't always the president's spouse. If a president is unmarried or widowed, another family member steps into the role. For example, THOMAS JEFFERSON'S wife passed away before he was sworn in as president in 1801. His daughter Martha "Patsy" Jefferson Randolph filled the role for some time.

So far, there have only ever been First Ladies. But one day soon, a First Gentleman might grace the White House. Many First Ladies have helped bring change to the country. They support important causes and help raise awareness about key issues.

EDITH WILSON has been called a "secret president." She stepped in to make big decisions for the country after her husband, WOODROW WILSON, got sick in 1919.

ELEANOR ROOSEVELT, FRANKLIN D. ROOSEVELT'S wife, was nicknamed the First Lady of Radio. She made more than three hundred radio appearances during her time in the White House and even wrote a daily newspaper column.

JACQUELINE "JACKIE" KENNEDY became a cultural icon during her time as **JOHN F. KENNEDY'S** First Lady, and she worked to preserve and restore the White House.

ROSALYNN CARTER was one of **JIMMY CARTER'S** closest advisors. She sat in on important meetings and advocated for mental health.

NANCY REAGAN was **RONALD REAGAN'S** wife. She ran a Just Say No campaign against drugs, teaching young people that drugs can be harmful.

LAURA BUSH worked to improve child literacy. She was a champion of **GEORGE W. BUSH'S** No Child Left Behind Act to improve education and an advocate for teaching kids to read at an early age.

HiLLARY RODHAM CLiNTON directed health care policy under **BILL CLINTON**. She went on to become a senator and later served as secretary of state for President **BARACK OBAMA**. In 2016, Hillary Clinton was the first female presidential nominee of a major party.

THE PRESIDENT'S DREAM TEAM

When we think of the executive branch, we often think of the president. But there are a ton of people who give the president advice and help them carry out the duties of the office.

The president's **chief of staff** makes sure everything runs smoothly. There are **speechwriters** and **policy advisors**. A **press secretary** updates the media on things happening in the White House, so the media can inform the people.

The president also works closely with their **cabinet**. No, it's not the place where you store things! This cabinet is a group of the president's closest advisors who help them make decisions. Cabinet members are selected by the president and approved by the Senate.

Each cabinet member leads a department of the executive branch and is known as a secretary (with one exception). Originally, there were four cabinet positions, which all still exist today.

The **SECRETARY OF STATE** is the top foreign affairs advisor to the president and the lead cabinet member.

The **SECRETARY OF THE TREASURY** runs the department that deals with money and the economy.

The **SECRETARY OF DEFENSE** protects national security and oversees the armed forces. (They were actually called the Secretary of War until 1947.)

The **ATTORNEY GENERAL** is the top law enforcement officer of the United States. Today, they're also the leader of the Department of Justice, which was created in 1870.

Over the years, eleven more presidential advisors have been added to the cabinet.

The **SECRETARY OF THE INTERIOR** is in charge of public lands and Native American affairs.

The **SECRETARY OF AGRICULTURE** helps farmers and protects our nation's forests.

The **SECRETARY OF COMMERCE** promotes economic growth and creates new jobs.

The **SECRETARY OF LABOR** keeps working people safe and healthy.

The **SECRETARY OF HEALTH AND HUMAN SERVICES** conducts research and deals with disease outbreaks.

The **SECRETARY OF HOUSING AND URBAN DEVELOPMENT** creates affordable housing for Americans.

The **SECRETARY OF TRANSPORTATION** is in charge of highways, plane travel, and other forms of transportation.

The **SECRETARY OF ENERGY** promotes conservation and alternative sources of energy.

The **SECRETARY OF EDUCATION** works to improve the country's schools.

The **SECRETARY OF VETERANS AFFAIRS** provides support for the people who served in the US military.

The **SECRETARY OF HOMELAND SECURITY** runs the Secret Service and works to prevent terrorist attacks.

IT'S A FACT

What if something happens to the president? Well, each cabinet member has a specific place on a long list of people who would take over as commander-in-chief. This is called the **order of sucession**. Cabinet members come after the vice president, the Speaker of the House, and the president of the Senate. (But we've never had to go past the VP on the list!)

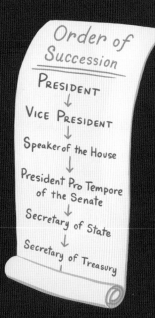

Order of Succession

PRESIDENT
↓
VICE PRESIDENT
↓
Speaker of the House
↓
President Pro Tempore of the Senate
↓
Secretary of State
↓
Secretary of Treasury
↓

NOBODY'S ABOVE THE LAW

The president of the United States might be super powerful, but they're not a superhero—and they're not above the law. The president is just a regular human. And humans sometimes make mistakes or do bad things.

The Founding Fathers knew what it was like to live under a corrupt king, and they didn't want the United States to fall into bad hands. So, they included presidential **IMPEACHMENT** in the Constitution. Impeachment is the idea that if the president (or another elected official) does something bad—like commit a crime or abuse their power—they can be removed from office.

Here's what the Constitution says about impeachment:

> "The President . . . shall be removed from Office on Impeachment for . . . Treason, Bribery, or other high Crimes and Misdemeanors."

Here's how impeachment works: First, the House of Representatives formally charges the president. The majority of representatives have to agree on the charge. If they do, the Senate holds a trial. It's run by the chief justice of the Supreme Court. In the end, the senators make the final decision on whether a president is guilty and should be removed from office.

That's a lot of steps! But impeachment is a serious matter, and everyone wants to make sure the president is following the rules.

Three presidents have been impeached in US history. So far, no president has been removed from office because of an impeachment trial. But it might happen one day if a president abuses their power. And even after leaving office, presidents can still face civil or criminal charges.

Here are the presidents who have been impeached:

ANDREW JOHNSON was impeached in 1868. Congress thought he was unfit to lead. He was just one vote short of being removed from office.

BILL CLINTON was impeached in 1998. He told a lie while being investigated, and that violates the oath he took as president.

DONALD TRUMP was impeached twice. He was first impeached in 2019 for abusing his power and blocking Congress from investigating him. Then in 2021, he was impeached for encouraging an uprising at the Capitol.

IT'S A FACT

In 1974, President **RICHARD NIXON** faced impeachment for abusing power and covering up a crime. To avoid being impeached, he resigned, or stepped down from office. His vice president, **GERALD FORD**, completed the rest of his term.

LIFE AFTER OFFICE

After four (or eight!) years of leading the country, it's time for the president to step down and make way for the next president to take over. What's on tap for a president after they leave office? First, a breather. Many presidents go on a much-needed vacation. Then former presidents have done a number of things with their lives after leaving the White House.

Some stay in government. WILLIAM HOWARD TAFT became a Supreme Court Justice. ANDREW JOHNSON served as a senator. JOHN QUINCY ADAMS was elected to the House of Representatives.

Some take on projects to help the world. JIMMY CARTER worked as a carpenter helping to build houses for the poor. He and several former presidents have gone on to create their own organizations to help tackle many of the world's biggest problems (like equality and global health).

And some pick up hobbies just for fun. GEORGE W. BUSH took up portrait painting. And DWIGHT D. EISENHOWER became a cattle farmer.

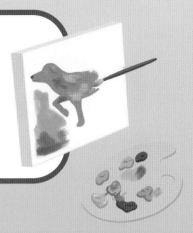

Many go on to document their legacy. Several former presidents have written books about their lives. Some have opened presidential libraries and museums containing documents and artifacts from their lives and time in office.

Former presidents continue to get perks of the office for the rest of their lives. They make a salary of about $200,000 each year. The Secret Service continues to protect them for life. And they don't have to pay for postage when they mail things.

★ YOUR VOTE MATTERS! ★

YOU CAN MAKE A DIFFERENCE

Just because you can't vote before you're eighteen doesn't mean you aren't a super powerful force in our democracy. There are so many things you can do to shape the future while you're still a kid!

GET INFORMED.

Learn about the candidates, read about the issues, and discover more about how our government works.

VOLUNTEER FOR A CAMPAIGN.

Go with a grown-up to knock on doors, make phone calls, or hand out buttons and fliers.

ATTEND A PROTEST.

Make a sign and grab a grown-up and a group of friends to march for what's right. If there isn't a march nearby, host one of your own!

DONATE MONEY.

Host an event like a lemonade stand to raise money for a candidate's campaign.

RUN FOR CLASS PRESIDENT.

It's a great way to practice democracy! Figure out what changes your classmates want to see, then launch your campaign.

TALK TO PEOPLE.

You might not agree with everyone's views and beliefs, but you can still try to understand where others are coming from.

ENCOURAGE GROWN-UPS TO VOTE.

Make sure the adults in your life check their voter registration status—and remind them to get out and vote on Election Day!

FIND OUT WHEN YOU CAN REGISTER TO VOTE.

Some states let you register to vote when you're as young as sixteen years old. Look into your state's voting rules. Then let your countdown to voting begin!

PRESIDENTS
OF THE UNITED STATES

1. GEORGE WASHINGTON: No political party, 1789–1797

2. JOHN ADAMS: Federalist, 1797–1801

3. THOMAS JEFFERSON: Democratic-Republican, 1801–1809

4. JAMES MADISON: Democratic-Republican, 1809–1817

5. JAMES MONROE: Democratic-Republican, 1817–1825

6. JOHN QUINCY ADAMS: Democratic-Republican, 1825–1829

7. ANDREW JACKSON: Democrat, 1829–1837

8. MARTIN VAN BUREN: Democrat, 1837–1841

9. WILLIAM HENRY HARRISON: Whig, March–April 1841

10. JOHN TYLER: Whig, 1841–1845

11. JAMES K. POLK: Democrat, 1845–1849

12. ZACHARY TAYLOR: Whig, 1849–1850

13. MILLARD FILLMORE: Whig, 1850–1853

14. FRANKLIN PIERCE: Democrat, 1853–1857

15. JAMES BUCHANAN: Democrat, 1857–1861

16. ABRAHAM LINCOLN: Republican, 1861–1865

17. ANDREW JOHNSON: Democrat, 1865–1869

18. ULYSSES S. GRANT: Republican, 1869–1877

19. RUTHERFORD B. HAYES: Republican, 1877–1881

20. JAMES GARFIELD: Republican, March–September 1881

21. CHESTER A. ARTHUR: Republican, 1881–1885

22. GROVER CLEVELAND: Democrat, 1885–1889

23. BENJAMIN HARRISON: Republican, 1889–1893

24. **GROVER CLEVELAND:** Democrat, 1893–1897

25. **WILLIAM MCKINLEY:** Republican, 1897–1901

26. **THEODORE ROOSEVELT:** Republican, 1901–1909

27. **WILLIAM HOWARD TAFT:** Republican, 1909–1913

28. **WOODROW WILSON:** Democrat, 1913–1921

29. **WARREN G. HARDING:** Republican, 1921–1923

30. **CALVIN COOLIDGE:** Republican, 1923–1929

31. **HERBERT HOOVER:** Republican, 1929–1933

32. **FRANKLIN D. ROOSEVELT:** Democrat, 1933–1945

33. **HARRY S. TRUMAN:** Democrat, 1945–1953

34. **DWIGHT D. EISENHOWER:** Republican, 1953–1961

35. **JOHN F. KENNEDY:** Democrat, 1961–1963

36. **LYNDON B. JOHNSON:** Democrat, 1963–1969

37. **RICHARD NIXON:** Republican, 1969–1974

38. **GERALD FORD:** Republican, 1974–1977

39. **JIMMY CARTER:** Democrat, 1977–1981

40. **RONALD REAGAN:** Republican, 1981–1989

41. **GEORGE H. W. BUSH:** Republican, 1989–1993

42. **BILL CLINTON:** Democrat, 1993–2001

43. **GEORGE W. BUSH:** Republican, 2001–2009

44. **BARACK OBAMA:** Democrat, 2009–2017

45. **DONALD TRUMP:** Republican, 2017–2021

46. **JOE BIDEN:** Democrat, 2021–

GLOSSARY

absentee voting: the process of voting in an election (usually by mail) when you cannot vote in person on Election Day

amendment: a change that is made to a bill or law

ballot: the paper, ticket, or screen used to vote in an election

cabinet: a group of people who give advice to the leader of a government

campaign: a series of actions done by someone running in an election to try to win

candidate: a person who is running for office and trying to be elected

caucus: a series of meetings where local members of a political party discuss the people in their party running for office and pick who they want to run for president

conservative: the political belief that the government's power should be limited and things should be kept more as they were in the past

constitution: a document that lists the laws of the United States and explains how it will be run

delegate: a person sent to represent others at the national conventions

democracy: a form of government in which the people choose their leaders with elections

elector: a voter chosen to represent a state in the US Electoral College system

Electoral College: a group of people chosen from each US state who meet to elect the president based on the votes cast by the people in those states

federal: of or relating to the central (or national) government

gerrymandering: changing the boundaries of a voting district in a way that favors one political party or group over another

impeachment: the process of bringing formal charges against a public official who may have committed a crime or abused their power while in office

inauguration: the ceremony to swear in a new president or another public official

lame-duck period: the time period after a presidential election and before a new president is sworn into office

liberal: the political belief that the government should take an active role in supporting change

national convention: a meeting of a political party, especially to nominate a candidate from that party for president

nomination: an official suggestion or selection of someone to run for office

political party: a group of people who hold the same views about how the government should run

polling place: a building or location where people go to vote in an election

poll: a way of predicting the outcome of an election by asking a smaller group of people who they voted for

popular vote: the majority number of votes received by a candidate based on the country's total number of voters

president-elect: the winner of a presidential election who has not been sworn into office yet

primary: an election to choose which candidate from a political party will run for president

suffrage: the right to vote in elections

swing state: a US state where Democrats and Republicans have similar levels of support

veto: the power or right of a president to reject a bill and prevent it from becoming a law

INDEX

Page numbers in *italics* refer to illustrations and photographs.

absentee voting, 72, 108
Adams, John, 23, 29, *29*, 35, 106, *106*
Adams, John Quincy, 23, 84–85, 102, 106
amendments, 9, 15–16, 108
Arthur, Chester A., 35, 106

ballots, 5, 70–71, 108
Biden, Joe, 22, *22*, 34, 49, 87, 93, 107
Black voters, 16–18, *18*, 65–66
blue states, 81
Buchanan, James, 106
Bush, George H. W., 23, *23*, *89*, 93, 107, *107*
Bush, George W., 13, 23, *23*, 85–86, 95, 103, 107
Bush, Laura, 95, *95*

cabinet, 96–99, 108
campaign issues, 55–58
campaign slogans, 44–45
campaigns, 41–49, 108
candidates, 24–26, 58–59, 108
Carter, Jimmy, 95, 102, 107
Carter, Rosalynn, 95, *95*
caucus, 25, 29–31, 108
citizenship, 14, 20
Cleveland, Grover, 22, *22*, 85, 106
Clinton, Bill, 96, 101, 107
Clinton, Hillary, 51, *85*, 96, *96*
conservatives, 27, 108
Constitution, 8–9, 14–16, 108
Coolidge, Calvin, 35, *45*, 107

debates, 50–54
delegates, 38–40, 108
democracy, 4, 7, 108
Democrats, 26–31, 81

Dewey, Thomas, 87

Eisenhower, Dwight D., 103, 107
Election Day, 60–62
elections, 12, 24–25, 83–84
Electoral College, 42, 77–81, 86, 108
electors, 78, 108
Emhoff, Douglas, 37, *37*
executive branch, 10, 20–21

federal, 10–11, 108
Federalist Party, 29
Fillmore, Millard, 35, 106
First Lady, 94–96
Ford, Gerald, 35, 101, 107

Garfield, James, 106
gerrymandering, 68–69, 108
Gore, Al, *85*, 86
government, 6–9
Grant, Ulysses S., 106

Harding, Warren G., 107
Harris, Kamala, 34, *34*, 37, *37*
Harrison, Benjamin, 23, *23*, 85, 106, *106*
Harrison, William Henry, 23, *23*, 36, 45, 91, 106, *106*
Hayes, Rutherford B., 85, 106
Hoover, Herbert, 45, 107
House of Representatives, 11, 83–84

impeachment, 100–1, 109
inauguration, 89–91, 109

Jackson, Andrew, 84, *85*, 106
Jefferson, Thomas, 94, 106
Johnson, Andrew, 35, 101, *101*, 106
Johnson, Lyndon B., 35, *45*, 107

judicial branch, 10

Kennedy, Jacqueline "Jackie", 95, *95*
Kennedy, John F., 54, *54*, 95, 107
King, Martin Luther, Jr., 18, *18*

lame-duck period, 89, 109
legislative branch, 10
liberals, 27, 109
Lincoln, Abraham, 13, 106

Madison, James, 23, 106
mail-in voting, 72–73
McKinley, William, 107
Monroe, James, 106

national conventions, 38–40, 109
Nixon, Richard, 35, 54, *54*, 93, 101, 107
nominations, 32, 109

Obama, Barack, 21, 33, 93, 107, *107*

PACs and Super PACs, 49
Pierce, Franklin, 106
political parties, 26–31, *28*, 109
Polk, James K., 106
poll taxes, 65
polling places, 70, 74–75, *74–75*, 76, 109
polls, 48, 109
popular vote, 77, 84, 86, 109
president-elect, 87–90, 109
presidents
    about becoming, 20–23
    life after office, 102–3
    list of all, 106–7
    responsibilities of, 12, 92–93
primary, 25, 29–31, 109

Randolph, Martha Jefferson, 94
Reagan, Nancy, 95, *95*
Reagan, Ronald, 79, *79*, 89, 95, 107
red states, 81

Republicans, 26–31, 81
Roosevelt, Eleanor, 95, *95*
Roosevelt, Franklin D., 21, *21*, 23, 45, 95, 107, *107*
Roosevelt, Theodore, 22, *22*, 23, 35, 107, *107*

Senate, 11, 36
Speaker of the House, 11
State of the Union address, 93
suffrage, 15–17, 109 (*see also* women's suffrage)
Supreme Court, 11
swing states, 41–42, 79, 82, 109

Taft, William Howard, 102, 107
Taylor, Zachary, 23, 106
Tilden, Samuel J., *85*
Truman, Harry S., 13, 35, 87, *87*, 107
Trump, Donald, 45, 51, 85, 87, 101, *101*, 107
Tyler, John, 35–36, 106

Van Buren, Martin, 106
veto, 12, 109
vice president, 34–37
voter fraud, 71
voter registration, 14, 63
voter suppression, 64–69
voting, 61–62, 72–73, 104–5
voting age, 14, 19, *19*
Voting Rights Act (1965), 17–18

Washington, DC, 11, 20, 78
Washington, George, 29, 35, 91, 106
White House, 5, *10*, *20*, 24, 37, 89, 90, 92, 94–95, 96, 102
Wilson, Edith, 94, *94*
Wilson, Woodrow, 45, 94, 107
women's suffrage, 16, 18–19, *19*

To Margo and the next generation of voters.

—RK

Copyright © 2024 by Scholastic Inc.

All rights reserved. Published by Scholastic Inc., *Publishers since 1920*. SCHOLASTIC and associated logos are trademarks and/or registered trademarks of Scholastic Inc.

The publisher does not have any control over and does not assume any responsibility for author or third-party websites or their content.

No part of this publication may be reproduced, stored in a retrieval system, or transmitted in any form or by any means, electronic, mechanical, photocopying, recording, or otherwise, without written permission of the publisher. For information regarding permission, write to Scholastic Inc., Attention: Permissions Department, 557 Broadway, New York, NY 10012.

Library of Congress Cataloging-in-Publication Data
Names: Katzman, Rebecca, author. | Duda, Ellen, illustrator.
Title: Your vote matters : how we elect the US president / written by Rebecca Katzman ; illustrated by Ellen Duda.
Description: New York : Scholastic Inc., 2024. | Includes index. | Audience: Ages 7–10 years
Identifiers: LCCN 2023035032 | ISBN 9781339046495 (pb) | ISBN 9781339046501 (hbk) | ISBN 9781546116714 (ebk)
Subjects: LCSH: Presidents—United States—Election—Juvenile literature. | BISAC: JUVENILE NONFICTION / Social Science / Politics & Government | JUVENILE NONFICTION / People & Places / United States /
General Classification: LCC JK528 .K38 2024 | DDC 324.973—dc23/eng/20231107
LC record available at https://lccn.loc.gov/2023035032

ISBN 978-1-339-04649-5 (paperback)
ISBN 978-1-339-04650-1 (hardback)

10 9 8 7 6 5 4 3 2 1   24 25 26 27 28

Printed in China   38
First printing, May 2024

Photos ©: 18: Alpha Historica/Alamy Stock Photo; 19 top: Everett Collection/Shutterstock; 19 bottom: TheRegents of the University of California; 22 top: Image courtesy of the Franklin D. Roosevelt Presidential Library and Museum, Hyde Park, NY; 28 left: Jeff Greenberg/www.agefotostock.com; 28 right: AP Photo/ Haraz Ghanbari; 37 top: AP Photo/Pablo Martinez Monsivais; 37 center: Shutterstock; 37 bottom: MICHAEL REYNOLDS/EPA-EFE/Shutterstock; 54 left: AP Photo; 54 right: Bettmann/Getty Images; 79 bottom: Harry Langdon/Getty Images; 85 top left: National Portrait Gallery, Smithsonian Institution, gift of the Swedish Colonial Society through Mrs. William Hacker; 85 top right: National Portrait Gallery, Smithsonian Institution; 85 middle left: National Archives; 85 bottom right: Universal History Archive/ UIG/Shutterstock; 85 bottom left: Joseph Sohm/Shutterstock; 87 top: Paul Chinn/The San Francisco Chronicle/Hearst Newspapers/Getty Images; 87 bottom: Bettmann/Getty Images; 89: George Bush Presidential Library and Museum.

Book design by Ellen Duda